Selah
Poetry that Speaks

by
QuiNina J. Sinceno

SELAH, Poetry that Speaks

By QuiNina Sinceno

Copyright © 2017 by QuiNina J. Sinceno
Self-Published by QuiNina J. Sinceno
GDI Enterprises
Destrehan, LA

Edited by Melissa McDonald & Anitra Winfrey

All rights reserved.

All rights reserved worldwide. No part of this book may be reproduced, stored in a retrieval system, or transmitted in any form or by any means, for example, electronic, mechanical, photocopy, or recording without prior written permission of the publisher. The only exception is brief cited quotations in printed reviews.

Dedication

I dedicate this book to all of the poets and writers with a dream to make an impact through words and to the one who encouraged me to complete this project when I didn't realize it existed within me.

Table of Contents

Preface

Introduction Piece…Who Am I?

Image of Worship

Da' Streets

Silent Screams

Nose Wide Open

Itch for the Lost

Church High

Fish Out of Water

Shell

Prodigal by Nature

Contemplation of Jeremiah 29:11

Thank You, Your Honor

Not Just Words, Proverbs 25:11

Daughter of the King

Let Me Be Me

I Am Suicidal

Conclusion

Preface

Thank you for taking a moment to read a few pieces that I believe were inspired by God. The whole purpose of this book is to encourage, to shed the light of truth onto controversial areas, and to enjoy a few works of art that I've written from my personal perspective. All of the pieces are themed around Christ and having an intimate relationship with Him in some way or another.

Selah means to "pause and think on that" so...

Selah & Enjoy

Introduction Piece

Who Am I?

Paradigm, God gave me that name because He had a shift in mind

A shift that shakes your thinking, Ruffles your Feathers and Rattles your cages

With words sharper than two edges, harder than pavement, breaking up stony ground with one distinct sound

As I open my ear He speaks today

"Go get my people, don't let them go Astray!"

Image of Worship

The image of worship is not a posture we assume during a song

It's a choice to believe God when everything seems to be going wrong

True worship cannot be faked because it only comes from within

It doesn't disguise itself in a dressed up temple full of sin

Ya see true worship is birthed
Though some try to pretend
Lifting dirty hands repeatedly
When will this madness end?
And we begin to go after God again

In spirit and in truth is how it should be

Instead we've perfected our hypocrisy

A generation that has been convinced that it's ok to, lay, play, sip, slip, dip, and tip
It's even in our leadership

Maybe that's why we don't trip

Now don't be condemned I was once there too

But I beg you don't forfeit your anointing
Hell really ain't the place you wanna go

Besides God has much better plans for you
To be his chosen generation, a royal priesthood, a holy nation

A peculiar people is what he called you

Stop imitating the world; instead give them a reason to imitate you

Let your worship develop into salt, the kind that makes the lost thirsty

Changing the world through the image of worship, the image that becomes you when Christ is truly seen instead of the nastiness of flesh

That's what you are destined to do

Let the image of worship BE the Image of YOU

Da' Streets

So, when are we gonna take it to the streets, man like for real yo

Instead of sitting within these four walls shaking our heads, clapping our hands, and patting our feet to these wack beats

The only sound I want to hear is the pulse of a heart that has just died as a heart of sin, resurrecting to the new life of Christ that now lives within

That sound causes even the angels to rejoice

Quick question? Can your praise teams cause the angels in heaven to sing? Selah

So when, beyond these walls will the gospel go?

To every pimp, prostitute, drug dealer, fornicator, adulterer, junky, and homo

Since we profess Christ as being within us and we in Him

The world should be uncomfortable remaining in sin

But we as the body have yet to totally tap into He that lies within

So in the streets they stay as we remain in our box of brick and clay

The truth now on display

To give life it must be something you truly possess

When you truly have it you can't be like all the rest

In the comfort of a box is not where you belong

Taking it to the streets, dats what's up All Day Long

Silent Screams

I see a kingdom that's hurting
It shows up in their eyes

Blank stares during praise and worship,
are no longer a surprise

Like leaves blowing in the wind,
following every new fad and trend

Full of STYLE but an Absence of
SUBSTANCE

When does this madness end?
And we begin to seek out the
generations that are obviously hurting

Screaming from within, help me I've
been captured by sin, the guilt from my
past is eating at my soul, my childhood
felt like a hell hole, now that I'm older
it's even worse I feel like my life is just
one bad curse
Everything I touch manages to fail
GOD can't you see me, Preacher cant
you tell!?

It's in my eyes, my face, my demeanor
I'm Just a Shell harvesting pain…
Please help me, I don't want to go to hell

Ya' see there's a scream within me
Somebody please tell me who I am

But they can't, they can only affirm

So what do you do, where do you turn
When we're only concerned with
building bigger buildings, filled with
those who remain empty within

Seems as though Rhema no longer
shows her face in God's house

The type of deliverance that pulls you out
of depression, guilt, shame & sin

The kind that launches you into destiny,
a word that speaks to your spirit, giving
you a charge, a sense of identity that can
only come from your Creator the Lover
of your soul

Sweetheart, Shugga-foot, Honey Bun,
you were made in His image, so He's the
only one who knows who you are

The Answer is in Him

Please, Please, let Him Silence your
Screams Within…

Nose Wide Open

Never thought I'd fall so quickly, but
OMG I Love Him so!

He says I'm the Apple in His eye, the
only star in His sky,

The motion of His wind
An extension of His hands

The capturer of His thoughts, I'm always
on His mind,

His conversation, hmmm so divine

The king that's stolen my heart, by
Loving me right from the start

A love wider than the oceans and deeper
than the seas

He knows me, every sickness, and disease

When my heart cries He soothes its fears
and when my face rains He bottles my
tears

My desire for Him grows intensely
Like stage curtains I open up to let Him see
His intimacy impregnates me to carry His seed, now I shall believe despite our Love's adversities

His purpose fulfilled in me is our Destiny

Jesus I Love Him So, Christ the ONE I'll Never Let Go

Itch for the Lost

Jesus Christ the Lover of my soul

The only one who can make me whole?
Heal this disease

Calm the storm raging inside me
This pain I feel I can no longer hide

My heart aches for the people I see everyday
Sitting on the corners wasting away

Lord I want to speak to them but I don't know what to say

Will they listen or just walk away

Church High

Ya see church was once my Novocain, I took it every Sunday and Wednesday to temporarily numb my pain

Yet on Monday I would always return back to the horror stories of life

Back to facing the death of my countenance Tuesday Night, the hole in my chest, the place where a heart is supposed to be hemorrhaged until there was no life left in me

No convictions to check me,

Blew through Wednesday midweek hype, went by so fast it wasn't enough to wet my appetite

The church just tickled my eardrums, spiritually fondled my flesh, took me to an emotional high, a mental quick hit, sermons and exhortations spoken to justify the nastiness of my flesh, an A&B selection with a beat laced with the chronic hook of and R&B song on a

Friday night, right before I pretended the Holy Spirit had taken flight, giving me permission to rock his world all night

Ooops, did I forget about Thursday? That's usually the day from hell too, an alcoholic hangover spilled into work from the Wednesday night church-a-holic blues, I watched the depressing videos of what we call the NEWS, tried to reflect on what was preached but who was I kidding into my mind those words just never reached, so my heart remained empty and my spirit malnourished, dying from an anointing famine, a recession of the presence and Glory of God they hypocritically sang about,

That was my Thursday

Saturday the itch begins but it's not enough to pick up my bible

Unfortunately unlike heroine the true gospel of Christ never got into my blood stream causing an addiction that would

give me the ability to hear the blood of
my generation scream, from the dirt of
early deaths, and the air, living,
breathing, bleeding, heart cries,
I never received an impartation, or a
desire for meat, I just kept choking on
"watered down milk" fed through the
breast of unconsecrated flesh

I ingested the same toxins they partook
as the preacher stood before the GOOD
BOOK

Sunday after Sunday, I left the same,
Now I'm standing at the gates before
judgment,
GOD WHERE'S MY NAME?! Selah

Fish Out of Water

Like a fish out of water I gasp

For someone to grab me and throw me back

That's where I'm supposed to be

But somehow I've managed to get misplaced
Or was it that I just forgot to continue to seek Your face

Like a fish out of water away from family

The air is different here its making me choke
I'm losing my wind, when will this torture end?

When I was young I was told that one day this is how it would be

That one day I may leave to fulfill a greater destiny

A destiny to feed this creation called man by giving Him me

So today is the day I stand face to face
accepting purpose

That's to feed through a sacrificed
lifestyle, so simple it's deep

Allowing my flesh to die so that man can
eat from pure nutrients of prepared meat

Not processed by cliché but a Holy
Ghost marinated word from God

Like a fish out of water
It's Not Just a Façade

God let this cup pass from me

Shell

I see empty shells decorated in much style, clothed in a mirage of royalty

But something's missing
The shell is empty, there's an absence of substance

Such a tragedy

The sight of a church with no word, no anointing, no Holy Spirit, no prayer or deliverance

Makes my soul weep

God help us, we've forsaken your presence
Diluted your anointing to escape conviction
So no true deliverance takes place

The word of God never takes root
Going about as empty shells everyday
Full of style but an absence of substance

Substance that keeps you grounded when all hell breaks loose

Substance that raises within you, like rivers of living water it begins to speak I'm more than a conqueror; it's Christ who lives within me, the Holy Spirit who fills this empty shell of mine

He doesn't intend to just pass or stop by but he desires to dwell

I Shall be His HOUSE, His TEMPLE, His SHELL

Prodigal by Nature

If I stretch my hands to thee, promise me you won't abandon me

I'm too old to change my taste buds alone
My desire for carnality has been my consumption from the first day I opened my eyes to see

I've become drunk of the fetal waters of a sin that my unwed father committed

DNA has left me with strands of a recessive gene formulated to lay and play

My bone structure has been bent and designed in iniquity

I've been pushed by a canal Birthed by the flooded sins of my mother who just had to give in

There's been a void in my life since daddy left me, I wanted to come to you years ago

But when I looked in the mirror that morning I was reminded, that I was just, a…"hoe"

So instead of leaving him I got back into the bed
Deep inside I really wanted you to come rescue me, I even tried to make him see You in me, but he couldn't

The created image of You in me had been distorted by the naturalistic rebellion my hypocrisy

I compromised my destiny and aborted your plan as I continued to push away as you reached out your hand

I'm Afraid of the responsibilities of becoming your child

But there's nowhere else I want to go, at your feet is where I want to be

Removing the mask that covers the depression of my heart brings me such liberty

You've seen my nakedness, but I don't feel violated or ashamed

Your word washes me from the pains of my past, the dysfunctions of my future, and the fears of my today

I didn't know how much I needed you until now
I've missed out on all the days you would have sent your advice, and the comfort you send during dark nights

I've missed your presence tucking me in at night, and the aroma of your daily bread

To have known your voice would have kept me out of every stranger's bed

Somehow, your protection has caused my enemies to flee

For that I say Thank You Sir

As a result, I accept your offer of the redemption costs for the secret place you have prepared (by sending your Son) for me

I know it sounds greedy but I just have one plea

I'm ready now, will You Father Me?

Contemplation of Jeremiah 29:11

For I know the thoughts that I think towards thee?

God does your plan really have the powers to rescue me?

To deliver me from my insanity, hmm insanity, the act of repeating the same action but expecting different results

Thoughts of Peace? Man you trippin, have you seen these thoughts?

I almost blew a hole in my brain one day My thoughts spin like whirlwinds: "I can't pay this", "Eviction Notice", "Sick again", "What am I going to do", "I hate my life", "I ain't got no money for gas"

Sounds like chaos to me, where's the peace in that?

Not of Evil? I'm just doing what I do, ya heard me

He was giving it so I took it, how was I supposed to know he had an STD, he looked clean to me, lawd all those muscles blinded me
To give me an Expected End? Don't we all just end up in the grave? God what are you saying to me? Huh? Destiny?! What is that?
A plan you have for me? Didn't I just say I ain't got no plans...unless you're talking about eating this food they done fixed after church, that's the only plan I've got, a sista hungry right na'

I know you're God and all but you must not know me, cuz I cuss, smoke a lil weed, get ma drink on, have a lil sex, ya know I gotta go clubbin, I gets my swag on regularly

Wow... you mean to tell me you still have better plans for me?

But I tried God, I tried to do it your way, but rebellion has become my curse and resistance my enemy every time I've gone after this thing you call Destiny

Ok God, whatever You say, I ain't got nothing to lose anyway, so I guess today is the day

Promise you'll never leave me
Fill this Void, this emptiness I feel everyday…ok here Goes Destiny
Here I come God, I'm walking Your Way

There's a part in me that, in the midst of all that I have going on is still unfulfilled, I keep trying to fill it but this Void just won't go Away!

That's why I do what I do

So, you're saying I'm unfulfilled because I'm really actually living without you? Let everything Go? Why I gotta let stuff Go? The other church folk are doing both, they seem like they're having fun

Ya girl over there in the choir was clubbin with us last night, she looked fulfilled to me with all that shoutin

Chosen? I'm chosen for What?! Royalty? Man, this ain't the bible days, Look, I want to come back to you, I really do, but, if I walk down that isle what would my friends do, what will they think if I become a Jesus Freak? Will you teach me?

Real talk, I'm really tired of this double lifestyle, it's just easy to pretend I'm ok

Thank You, Your Honor

Now faith is the substance of things hoped for, the evidence of things not seen

If I don't wear the type of attire you'd like could you not see the evidence of God in me?

Is it my fault you've chosen to believe I have no substance because you can't get past me, to see me, so who's really in their flesh?

I guess that's why India said "I'm not my hair"

My cultured style seems to have threatened your religion

But I'm free enough to know, self reflection may be the way to go

If I'm judged by my appearance, then what does it really say?

Does my representation match whom I represent?

Am I a mirror of His image? When you see me can you see His face?

Or am I just a mirage of God's grace?

I have the look but don't get too close, there's no substance, I really don't spend any time in the Book

Nawl, hold up, on second thought…

When was the last time you took a look?

If you were cross examined, would your sentence be lethal injection?

I think your heart has an infection, He didn't say Love only Perfection

Love all, was His direction, it was love that brought hope to what had not yet been seen

Keep watching though, the evidence of His faith in me, NOW will Appear

Thank you, your honor for nominating yourself

Writing me off built strength in me, I even appreciate how you belittled my anointing and disrespected my deliverance

Because you couldn't receive a message stuck on how I delivered it, you missed your deliverance

But it's ok others got it though

As for you, your honor, I pray you let that go

Don't miss Christ looking for a Religious Freak Show

Not Just Words, Proverbs 25:11

For the words that I speak they are spirit and they are life

Like an artist painting a canvas we design our lives through this microphone of a mouth piece

Sounds from the symphony played by the horns of vocal chords through the force of lungs, an inspired transmission of heart, interpreted by brain waves

What type of songs do we play?

What we say births the destiny of realities in our future and our today

So speak words that put every generational demonic curse to flight

Then every time you pray, speak prophetically pulling the destiny blessings of your tomorrow into your today

Lord give us this day our daily bread, it's imperatively crucial that you know what to say

Without it as a leaf of an erratic blow, conforming into the latest trend, an absence of identity camouflaged by a dysfunctional society, off you go

Convinced that it's ok to just go with the flow, a Godless mentality that forces destructive catastrophic words to be released from a heart full of misdirected priorities and deceit

Brothers and Sisters don't sit and watch what you say create a satanic mirage of fulfillment through the sins of this world when God's word gives you a clear image of the One that can be touched by your infirmities

The One who has given you an expected end, you're not just a leaf in the wind

Speak what God says, speak yourself into the prosperity of destiny, don't faint

Let the words of my mouth and the meditation of my heart be acceptable in thy sight oh Lord my strength and my redeemer.

I Speak Life…Selah

Daughter of the King

Dear Daughter,
My heart bleeds for you

I've watched you dress yourself in layers to hide the fact that you're bleeding too

You have yet to embrace what I've sent your brother to do

Baby girl, the luggage of your past is too heavy for you

This bottle in my hand it over flows, your tears of the night it can no longer hold

Silent depression and camouflaged oppression has made your house cold, leaving you with a self-esteem that has fallen into a black hole

Your smile has become an eclipse, your laugh a falling star

Daughter why won't you let me show you who you are

Why choose poverty when you were born rich
Your name is not B with an itch
Your worldly carnal addictions like crack have replaced your itch for me

You've turned your ear to the darkness of daylight, danced to the sounds of sin, fulfilling the lust of your flesh that burned within

You ate from the tree of deception
Eve's curse multiplied in generational reception

My dearest daughter your eyes are scaled
Satan my enemy has tried to steal you away blindly

He's ripped you off repeatedly because you can't see

Death is his charge to play, your sin is where his calculations begin

Though, he's fostered you into his family you're not born of his blood

The seed of my words formed you, the thoughts that I think have kept you, the blood of your brother Christ shed for you is waiting to cover you

I've already sent Him to redeem you
It's your gift to accept, He's hidden now but you'll find Him in 180° (degrees) He will lead you back home to me

To see my face you'll have to wait, but I'll meet you at the gate of eternity

As a daughter of the king there are tasks you must fulfill

In my book you'll find My Will, in spirit and truth is how you worship me

In my presence you will be

Remember daughter, I love you,
Sincerely
Your Father. GOD

Let Me Be Me

Don't make me feel like dirt because my attire is beneath you

It's all I got right now!

So what do you expect me to do? I'm not hiding anymore…

This is Just who I am!

What if my skirt was long but I lifted it for every man that comes along

What if all of my shirts covered my chest, But every night there was a stranger's head resting on my breast

Something isn't right, is it really that serious to look just right?

I don't want to look the part, that's where all the stereotypes of self-righteousness start and judgmental-ism takes place, making me unapproachable by the common face

God is this really necessary?

I don't want anyone to be intimidated by the way I dress
That's what I remember, fancy suits used to terrify me because they accompany a cold look

No smiles, hugs, or embraces so I never spoke up when I was in pain

You know I'm not rebellious, but this feels insane

Feels like you're stripping my liberty, Freedom was beginning to be my Name

I Am Suicidal

Chosen to die an early death
Daily as I take each breath

Exhaling every toxin of my past
Shanked by a sword with two edges

I Am Suicidal

I've chosen to kill everything in me that does not please the Father of eternity

So off the cliff I jump and into the water I leap

If I survive long enough they say the waters would drown me, flowing continuously into my belly, when I exhale it comes out of me, the deeper I go the more the glory will show

Just have to get into the flow, this mentality of being as a leaf in the wind has got to go

Standing firm, planted near rivers of living water is the aim

I've decided to be Surrounded by those who've decided to reproduce fruit, leaving the gang in those cheap sheep suits, Because they're Nourished by worship, in their spirit lies truth

They've been tatted by script, Psalms 1 stamped across the left breast

Since My heart leaked of corruption I decided to let it drain

Filled it with new blood, a donated transfusion from a new donor, Christ is His name

In my memory shall this day remain?

The day I killed my flesh and denounced my name

Just in case you've never met Christ I pray you were introduced through this book.

There are lots of problems that we have to face today, many situations come our way, and circumstances that can't be explained

We deal with test and trials of faith, even experience pain and heart ache

But there's one thing I'm sure that remains true, and that God has amazing plans for you

If you haven't I encourage you to give Him your life today and if you have I pray you trust, depend, and grow in love with Him more and more each day

He's the answer to everything we face
It's in His word that we see His face

Life without Christ is a life without peace and unfulfilled

When I encountered Him He gave me peace and enlightened me to a purpose I didn't know I had

So if you will, I invite you to pray with me.

Father we thank you for granting us peace for every storm we have to face and for the strength to endure every test and trial through your grace. We thank you for sending your son Jesus Christ to save us from our sins by forfeiting His life, we accept His sacrifice and believe that now He lives in heaven as well as in us. We ask that you would continue to protect us, guide us and lead us through your Holy Spirit, as we grow closer to you. We thank you for loving us first and because of such we return with giving you our lives and dedicating ourselves to sharing that same love to those who have yet to experience it. In Jesus name, Amen

"For the words that I Speak, they are Spirit and they are Life"

Selah Poetry that Speaks
By QuiNina J. Sinceno

www.quininaj.com

Email: only1paradigm@gmail.com
Social media: @QuiNinaJ #Paradigm
@QuiNinaJSinceno

Additional published works:

Life of JOY: The Key to Transformed Living

www.ingramcontent.com/pod-product-compliance
Lightning Source LLC
Chambersburg PA
CBHW071222070526
44584CB00019B/3124